YOUR KNOWLEDGE HAS VALUE

Bibliographic information published by the German National Library:

The German National Library lists this publication in the National Bibliography; detailed bibliographic data are available on the Internet at http://dnb.dnb.de .

Imprint:

Copyright © 2018 GRIN Verlag
Print and binding: Books on Demand GmbH, Norderstedt Germany
ISBN: 9783668728974

This book at GRIN:

https://www.grin.com/document/425692

Jack Griffiths

Is America the biggest threat to international security?

GRIN Verlag

GRIN - Your knowledge has value

Since its foundation in 1998, GRIN has specialized in publishing academic texts by students, college teachers and other academics as e-book and printed book. The website www.grin.com is an ideal platform for presenting term papers, final papers, scientific essays, dissertations and specialist books.

Is America the biggest threat to international security?

Jack Griffiths - 3009

HAGLEY CATHOLIC HIGH SCHOOL

Abstract

My dissertation is a very topical issue at the moment – the geopolitical situation of the world at the moment. I have an interest in the surrounding world and in international diplomacy so I enjoyed writing my dissertation very much. I shall be evaluating the role of the U.N and the current state of play of international security. As in, is there a threat to international security, defining international security and how effective the U.N is at dealing with threats to international security. As the fore-front protector of international conflicts, it is important to understand and acknowledge what the U.N does.

I will be going through the aims and ambitions of each of the three nations. For example, I shall be look at the reasons for ISIS's actions within its caliphate and across the world. I shall also be looking into each country's nuclear policy and the current diplomatic relations between these countries and their biggest enemies, and outlining and possible problems, which may arise from these fractured relations.

I shall also be discussing human rights. More specifically, I shall be talking about America's international violations, for example, mistreatment of prisoners in Iraq and the various issues surrounding the notorious Guantanamo bay. I shall also be looking at forced labour camps in North Korea and the various mass slaughtering of civilians by ISIS. I shall also be looking at how America caused the threat of ISIS and other associated Muslim extremists, and so should be held accountable for any stemming actions of these groups. Human rights is a very topical issue and since it is deceleration has been the reason for foreign intervention, such as the U.K's current involvement in Syria.

Contents

Introduction

The question for I have chosen for my dissertation is: Is America the biggest threat to international security?

To anyone who watches the news, reads a newspaper, or goes on social media, it is clear that there is some sort of international issue arising at the moment which may be easily considered a threat to international security. This issue, which is apparently arising, is what is going to be the focus of my essay.

In this essay, I shall be explaining and evaluating the current international climate, and I will define exactly what international security means. Furthermore, I shall also be concluding whether or not there is a threat to international security, and if there is, who is the biggest threat – whether it comes from America, ISIS or North Korea.

The main contributors to these new international tensions are; the emerging caliphate of ISIS currently operating in Iraq and Syria predominantly; the Democratic People's Republic of Korea (DPRK), also known as North Korea; and the United States of America (who I shall mostly refer to as the U.S in this dissertation). Each of these states- if you count ISIS as a state- regularly violate human rights- such as torture or minority discrimination, commit war crimes and other such international crimes supposedly enforced by the U.N. In this dissertation, I shall be looking at the attempts to keep the peace by the U.N, and perhaps why these attempts have failed in the past, and therefore whether or not they will fail in the future to prevent another large-scale international war.

Another big concern currently is nuclear weapons. America has the biggest nuclear arsenal in the world and has the largest annual budget for their military, bigger than what the next five top spending countries on their military budgets are in the world put together. America is, however, in the non-nuclear proliferation treaty. North Korea on the other hand has recently pulled out. This clearly shows that North Korea is gearing up for some conflict. Furthermore, just because America has agreed to non-nuclear proliferation, it does not necessarily mean that they would not use their nuclear weapons.

This topic is extremely relevant at the moment, due to all of the attention received by North Korea and America regarding their possible violations, is regarding the very

3

important issue of human rights. It is especially relevant concerning all of the terror attacks currently plaguing Europe and the Middle East, as well as the large number of people imprisoned a Guantanamo bay by the U.S indefinitely.

In my conclusion, I will conclusively draw on who, from the result of my research in my dissertation, is considered the biggest threat to international security. However, this may not necessarily be the U.S as at the moment it could easily be either of the other two predominate agitators.

Chapter 1: International security: The State of Play

Chapter 1.1 What is international security?

According to the oxford dictionary definition, security is "The state of being free from danger or threat." (Oxford Dictionary, Originally 1884). The oxford dictionary is a very reliable source as it has been around for half a century and has been widely used and reviewed across the world many times. For this reason, its definitions cannot be refuted by another source.

Therefore, for people to feel secure on an international scale, people all across the world must feel secure. Most people, by this definition will most probably not feel this way. Whether it be the threat from of a nuclear apocalypse due to a war between the North Koreans and the Western World, or America's constant meddling in international politics, or the threat of terrorism from the caliphate of ISIS currently operating predominantly in Iraq and Syria, most citizens of the world will agree that there is some sort of threat or issue regarding their international security.

Another possible way to explain international security is whether people feel secure when visiting a foreign country. It is the case that many foreign nationals who visit places like Iraq and Syria where ISIS are currently operating will not feel very secure because they are international citizens. The case is similar in North Korea, where a western person would be treated very suspiciously, as if they were a spy, and the North Korean government (DPRK) had recently not guaranteed the security of foreign nationals in their country. In such cases, people would not feel very secure as international visitors.

Chapter 1.2 The role of the UN

The United Nations (U.N) is thought of by many people around the world to be the biggest and possibly the most effective agency in existence responsible for keeping the international situation secure. In this sub-chapter, I shall be looking at whether or not this really is the case, and how effective the U.N might be in the case of a serve international crisis.

The U.N has a delegation called the Security Council, whose sole purpose and interest is to tend to for and maintain international security. It has 15 Members, and each Member has one vote. Under the Charter of the U.N, all Member States are obligated to comply with Council decisions. The role of the Security Council is that it takes the lead in determining whether there is a threat to the international security. It calls upon the nations involved in the dispute to settle it by peaceful means. In some cases, however, the Security Council can resort to imposing sanctions or even authorize the use of force to maintain or restore international security.

However, the issue with the security council in its current climate is that it may not be in the most effective state to deal with the growing problems, such as the caliphate of ISIS or in fact the United states of America.

The reason for this probable ineffectiveness is down to the fact that ISIS is not actually a state, and therefore is not a member of the U.N. This means that the U.N. is powerless to impose economic sanctions on ISIS. Military force is the only option, however other members of the U.N would disagree with this action as military action by the U.N may end up doing more harm to regular citizens in Syria and Iraq, and it is difficult to distinguish between a Syrian rebel and a member of ISIS.

The second reason for this probable inefficiency with dealing with certain issues, such as those involving the USA, is that the USA is a leading member of the UN. In the case of military supporting being needed, most will come from the USA. If the issue concerns them, they would not send troops against themselves and so the UN would be left with very little military support. However, the Security Council could overcome this problem, if they manage to persuade other military pacts, such as the North Atlantic Treaty Organisation, or the Economic Community of West African States. However, this would be extremely difficult due to the large influence that the U.S has in the world and the formidable size of its army, navy and air force, and its huge military arsenal.

On the other hand, the U.N has successfully dealt with many threats to international security in the past, such as from 2005–2011, when United Nations Mission in the Sudan (UNMIS) in Sudan during the Second Sudanese Civil War stopped the worsening of the situation.

Chapter 1.3 Is there a threat to international security?

I am strongly of the opinion that there is a threat to international security.

The biggest indicator that there is a threat to international security is that we have set up an international organisation to protect international security and deal with any threats to it – the U.N. Security council. If there were no threats to international security the presence of such an organisation would not be necessary in our world.

A recent survey conducted by ComRes for the Independent found that 46% of adult British voters "are more concerned about Kim Jong-un's secretive state than the Syrian civil war, which ISIS has exploited to expand and us as al launch pad for global terror acts." (Dearden, 2017)[1] With only 22% of respondents saying that Syria was a greater threat. This clearly shows that in general the British population believe that there is a threat to international security, and that they believe North Korea is that threat.

An issue with this survey is that it does not deal with security on an international scale, as it only asks the opinion of British citizens. A Survey conducted in 2013/2014 by Gallup International and published on BrilliantMaps.com; found that "The US was the overwhelming choice - 24% of respondents - for the country that represents the greatest threat to world peace today." (Hammer, 2017)[2] This clearly contradicts Dearden's results who found North Korea to be a bigger threat to international security.

However, both of these surveys clearly show that people do clearly feel that there is a threat, whether it comes from the U.S or North Korea to international security. On the contrary, the results would suggest that there is indeed a threat to international security.

---

[1] This source is reliable as ComRes is an independent and professional organisation who regularly conduct polls across the UK meaning their sampling would be good and there should be little, if any, political bias. The independent is also a relatively unbiased newspaper and so the results should be reliable. However, this poll was conducted straight after a nuclear test by the DPRK. If the poll was conducted after a terrorist attack by ISIS, perhaps the results would have been different.

[2] Hammer's publication of the Gallup International survey is highly reliable as Gallup International is again an independent research organisation and all research is conducted in strict adherence to the ICC/ESOMAR International Code of Marketing and Social Research Practices. This means their results are highly reliable. However, the issue with the research is that it was conducted a number of years ago meaning that the results may not be applicable to the current international climate.

Chapter 2: Aims and ambitions

Chapter 2.1 The aims of ISIS

The new caliphate of ISIS emerging in Iraq and Syria has many names; IS (Islamic state), ISIL (Islamic state of Iraq and the Levant) and ISIS (Islamic state of Iraq and Syria). For the purpose of my dissertation, I shall be referring to this caliphate as ISIS.

To establish whether America is the biggest threat to international security, we should first establish the aims of ISIS on an international level, and then make a judgement based on that whether ISIS is a bigger threat than America.

According to an article published in the *Independent* in 2017 ISIS, have six main aims:

1. To expand in Europe
2. To consolidate their rule
3. To establish an effective state

4. To rule the world

5. To challenge the great enemies of the past e.g. Rome and Persia
6. To reach a generation of Muslims

(Danny Romero, 2017)[3]

If the aforementioned aims are in fact true, and ISIS is currently trying to achieve them, then this would suggest that ISIS are a bigger threat to international security. The first aim, 'to expand in Europe' would involve the deaths of hundreds of thousands, if not millions of people. This of course undoubtedly threatens international security. The second and third aims, 'to consolidate their rule and establish an effective state,' would mean they would have to illegally seize land from Iraq and Syria- which they currently believe is theirs – and establish trade, government and an economy. This does not pose a huge international threat, only to

---

[3] The source may be unreliable as it was written for a newspaper, all of which have different agendas to promote, depending on the political affiliation of the owners and editors. In addition to this, the article was published in 2015 and so the aims of ISIS may have changed in the last three years, meaning the source may be invalid. However, ISIS is continuing to act as it did in 2015 so the source is most likely still valid.

those countries in its vicinity. However, in relation to their fourth aim, 'to rule the world', that would clearly pose a huge threat to international security, and would violate the purpose of the U.N and many of the Human rights, such as; free speech; freedom of movement; Freedom from Interference with Privacy, Family, Home and Correspondence; and in accordance with their sixth aim, 'to reach a generation of Muslims', which would violate the freedom of religion and the right to a fair and free world.

Clearly, the aims of ISIS would suggest that they are a huge threat to international security. However, I, like many others observing the geo-political scene, seriously doubt ISIS's capacity to carry out their aims, and therefore I doubt the level of threat faced by the international community from ISIS.

Chapter 2.2 Reasons for ISIS's actions

In this chapter, I shall be exploring the possible reasons why ISIS hate the west and therefore why they insist on being a threat to international security.

According to an article published on the mirrors website, there are six main reasons why ISIS hate the west. These are: Because you are disbelievers; because you are liberal; because you are atheist; for your crimes against Islam; for your crimes against Muslims; for invading our lands. (Evans, 2017)[4] These reasons are apparently big enough for the estimate number of 200,000 militants in ISIS's militia to kill hundreds of thousands of innocent people and to risk their own lives. However, the Qur'an states: "Kill the idolaters wherever you find them, and capture them, and blockade them, and watch for them at every lookout..." (Quran 9:5)(This is a highly reliable source as it comes from the holy scripture of Islam itself, meaning it can certainly be trusted). This is where most of jihadist militant groups, along with ISIS, justify and carry out those actions. Despite this, it is a poor and misinterpreted excuse used by these extremists. "Idolaters" and "unbelievers" are specific in nature and are not general commands for the murder of all those who refuse to accept

---

[4] The source is unreliable as it is a newspaper article from a right-wing newspaper, with its own separate agenda, which it is pushing. However, The authors gets their information from a statement already released by ISIS, which makes it a lot more reliable than if it was just a newspaper article, as it comes from ISIS themselves.

Islam as their way of life. In addition, ISIS regularly kill Muslim's, the very people they are supposed to be looking out for and protecting.

On the international scene, ISIS cannot carry out their aims and will be never satisfy with their reasons for hating the west, as they would need to become a functioning state. For this, according to the United Nations Research Institute for Social Development, 5 things are necessary: Assist in the acquisition of new technologies, Mobilize and channel resources to productive sectors, Enforce standards and regulations, Establish social pacts, Fund deliver and regulate services and social programmes. While ISIS may be enforcing standards and regulations – on their ideology based on the Qur'an – it is failing to fulfil all of the other criteria, and therefore cannot be considered a state. Due to their limited capacity as simply a caliphate, their impact on international security is very limited.

Chapter 2.3 North Korean diplomatic relations

The result of the recent survey on international security suggested that North Korea was the country that most British voters were concerned by as demonstrated by the study published in the independent (Dearden, 2017). North Korea or the Democratic People's republic of Korea (DPRK), have recently been causing strife among the international community due to their supreme leaders, Kim Jong-Un, insistent on perusing a campaign of developing nuclear weapons. To determine whether North Korea is a threat to international security, we must look at the current diplomatic situation with the North Koreans and other world powers.

Anglo-North Korean relations have never been the strongest due to the Korean War; the United Kingdom has a poor relationship with the DPRK as they were on opposing sides. The UK is now, and has always been an ally of the United States, whereas the North Koreans are allied with China and Russia, who also have a poor relationship with the UK. This means that in the event of an international crisis, the UK and DPRK would most likely be on opposing sides.

However, this poor relationship does not necessarily mean that the North Koreans would threaten international security. Furthermore, in 2000, North and South Korean diplomatic relations began to improve slowly, meaning that improved relations were formed between North Korea and the UK. In addition, this year, North Korea opened an embassy in London clearly demonstrating the hugely improved relations between the two countries.

Despite this improvement in relations, however, in 2013 the DPRK advised the British Embassy in North Korea and all other countries that the safety of their citizens would not be guaranteed. This was due to the worsening of North Korean and South Korean relations. In 2016, the Deputy Ambassador of North Korea to the United Kingdom defected to South Korea with British officials due to the fear for their lives. (editors M. , 2017)[5] This does indicate a potential threat to the security of international citizens in North Korea. To determine the extent of this threat we must look at North Korean relations with another big player on the international scene: The United States of America.

The relationship between the U.S and the DPRK has always been poor. Firstly, it is down to the US's long standing hatred of communism and everything communist. An addition to this was the US's involvement in the Korean War, as a front of the cold war against the 'enemy' of communism. However, since the Korean War, the relationship between the US and the DPRK had been fairly stable, poor, but stable nonetheless. What caused the deterioration of this relationship was Kim-il Sung's insistence on perusing a policy of nuclear armament, which has continued to this day under Kim-Jong Un. An Inter-continental ballistic missile fired from the Korean peninsula could easily reach most major U.S states and cities.

A statistic from my research puts the number at only 9% of Americans, who have a favourable view of the North Koreans and 87% view the North Koreans in a bad light. (editors M. , 2017)[6]

Their distrust is not entirely unfounded; the North Koreans have been guilty of committing international crimes. For example: In 1994, they were found to be shipping SCUD missiles to Yemen, which was intercepted by Spanish soldiers. A

---

[5]This source has come from Wikipedia, which is an extremely commonly visited site with millions of users utilizing its resources every day. However, anybody can edit and change information on the site meaning that the information may be false or inaccurate. However, the source is generally reliable as most contributors quote their sources, proving the validity of what has been written

[6] Similarly, to the previous source, Wikipedia is in theory a reliable source and most information can be crossed checked for reliability, as those sources of information are quoted on the website. However, almost anybody can edit and add information to this page, they could put misinformation, which has not been fully verified, decreasing its reliability.

further offence in 1994 the US sent a helicopter to North Korea but it was shot and the North Koreans held the surviving passengers, refusing their release. But that's not all. In 2005, there were North Koreans producing fake American bank notes, which contributes to inflation, badly damaging the economy. (editors M. , 2017) Both these sources clearly agree that diplomatic relations between the DPRK and other countries are patchy, supporting the reliability of the argument that their poor relations could potentially cause a war.

However, the U.S has always had a very strong military presence in South Korea in order to put pressure on the North. This can be argued to lower the threat from the North, as they are aware they would be incapable of winning a war against such allies. On the other hand, it can also be argued that this pressure has increased the norths ambitions to create weapons of mass destruction, to avoid a war of attrition with these powers. What is clear is that there is a large threat from the DPRK to international security. The extent of this threat is unknown. The DPRK has only recently successfully tested one inter-continental ballistic missile capable of carrying a nuclear warhead. These have not yet been fully tested and are not able to be launched yet. Compare this to Russia's 396 missiles based in silos or mobile launchers, or America's 450 silo-based Minuteman III missiles, this is a comparatively small number, and would again suggest that it is perhaps America who is the bigger threat to international security. I shall look at this further in my next sub-chapter.

Chapter 2.4 the complexities of nuclear weapons

Although I have briefly looked at nuclear weapons in my previous chapter, I shall now look at the threat of nuclear weapons from the three main players of my dissertation. Nuclear weapons have long been the subject of protests and worry amongst the international security. Although only two nuclear weapons were ever used, their destructive powers have long since evolved past the now primordial bombs dropped on Hiroshima and Nagasaki.

Firstly, ISIS. Is there any threat from ISIS regarding nuclear weapons? Most likely not. They do not have the capabilities in any way to develop a nuclear weapons programme – mostly because this would require a functioning economy, which a caliphate does not have. The possibility of them stealing a nuclear warhead would also be very slim, as armies of well-trained and ruthless soldiers protect them. In the area that ISIS currently controls – lands in Syria in Iraq- there are also no nuclear weapons, meaning they would have to invade the likes of Turkey, Iran, Israel or Pakistan. In summary, there is an incredibly small chance that ISIS could gain access to missiles capable of carrying a nuclear warhead.

Then we come to the DPRK. As I have previously mentioned, the DPRK do not have the capability to facilitate a working inter-continental ballistic missile (ICBM) development programme, despite their single successful test of a ICBM, the Hwasong-15, in July 2017. They are however, very capable of hitting closer enemies, such as Japan or South Korea, with their shorter ranged missiles, such as the No-Dong or the Musudan DM-25. These capabilities do indicate a very real and ever-present threat to international security. However, it is extremely unlikely that the DPRK would launch these missiles, as the hitting a country like Japan or South Korea would cause more problems for them then the benefits it would bring. This is because these counties have some very powerful western allies, such as America, which has roughly 23,000 troops stationed in South Korea. The American also have an immense number of weapons of mass destruction comparatively. This therefore can be argued that the Americans are acting as a peacekeeping force in the Korean peninsula.

With this in mind, it is important to consider the Americans nuclear weapons policy. An official government website gives an overview of the nuclear policy of the U.S. The most important is that it is a U.S. goal to prevent nuclear weapons from ever being used, by either a state or a non-state actor, and that the sole purpose of U.S. nuclear weapons is providing deterrence for itself and its allies. (cited, U.S. nuclear weapon policy, 2009)[7] It is clear from this article that the American nuclear arsenal is entirely intended to be for peacekeeping purposes. The logic can be seen, by having the world's largest nuclear arsenal by about 50 silos', most countries would not attempt a ballistic attack against the U.S, as they would be massively outgunned, and would essentially be an unwinnable conflict. Clearly, as no country has fired

---

[7] This source is highly reliable as it comes from a '.org' website meaning it is official and approved by the government. However, as nuclear weapons are military weapons and so much of the information will be censored, through D-notices. There is also no author cited, throwing doubt on to the validity of the source.

nuclear weapons at another- apart from the U.S- this policy has been an effective and continues to this day. This peacekeeping policy would indicate that the U.S is not the biggest threat to international security.

Chapter 3: The horrific issue of human rights

Chapter 3.1 American and North Korean human rights violations

Since the United Nations General Assembly decreed the Universal Deceleration of Human Rights in 1948, most members of the UN have since tried to enforce their own laws on human rights. The Human Rights Council was set up in order to assess the state of human rights in the members of the UN.

America is perceived to be at the forefront of protected human rights and civil liberties. However, Amnesty internationals' summary of American civil liberties paint a far darker tale. Two years after a senate committee reported crimes in the secret C.I.A detention programme, there was still no accountability for crimes committed under international law. In August, the UN Human Rights Committee said that the US was obliged to investigate accusations into torture, which had not taken place. No action was taken to end impunity for the systematic human rights violations, including torture and enforced disappearances, committed by the C.I.A. Many of the detainees [at Guantanamo bay] were kept there 'indefinitely' without charge or trial. Indigenous women in the U.S were 2.5x more likely to be raped and there were gross inequalities for indigenous to access post rape care. (International, 2017)[8]This shows that the U.S is discriminatory to its own citizens, so how will it treat non-U. S citizens? Clearly, Citizens of their own country are very poorly treated, and the treatment of international citizens at Guantanamo bay is even worse. It is clear from this report that the U.S does pose a real threat to the security of international citizens.

North Korean violations on the other hand, are far worse. A 2014 UN Commission of Inquiry found that abuses in North Korea were without parallel in the contemporary world. They include extermination, murder, enslavement, torture, imprisonment,

---

[8] This source is fairly reliable as it is an independent human rights group, however this article doesn't state all the good that the U.S does for the advancement of human rights, meaning it is extremely biased. This, however, does not necessarily make it unreliable.

rape, forced abortions, and other sexual violence. North Korea operates secretive prison camps where perceived opponents of the government are sent to face torture and abuse, starvation rations, and forced labour. Fear of collective punishment is used to silence dissent. There is no independent media, functioning civil society, or religious freedom. (cited, North Korea, 2018)[9] These abominable acts are the result of an isolated nefarious totalitarian state, and are extremely inexcusable.

Both of these sources were released by the same independent organisation, and although they maybe be highly bias in which way they argue, they are reliable. They also allow for a comparison between the two countries, and from both sources, it is clear that the DPRK commits far more egregious human rights violations.

However, the extent of these actions are truly unknown. It is a similar case as to the American situation, if the DPRK is capable on systematic violations of its own people, how would they treat non-citizens? However, unlike the Americans, there has been no proof of the DPRK entrapping and abusing international citizens, such as in Guantanamo bay, again suggesting that the Americans may present a larger threat to international security.

Chapter 3.2 Actions of ISIS

The violation of Human Rights by ISIS is clear. They violate the right to life, the right to a fair trial, the freedom of thought, belief and religion and many others by persecuting people based purely on their beliefs, without a fair trial. These are clear violations of human's rights. Furthermore, as ISIS is not a state, it is conducting these atrocities on international citizens, such as those from Iraq and Syria, not to mention the numerous terrorist attacks conducted on sovereign land, proving that they may well be a bigger threat to international security.

The next issue regarding ISIS involves the U.S, and might be considered one of the most abominable moral acts in recent history. The U.S Vice-president, Joe Biden acknowledged that there was "No al-Qaida in Iraq until the US and Britain invaded." The US has also exploited the existence of ISIS against other forces in the region as

---

[9] This source is very reliable. It gets all of its information from official inquiries by the U.N. It is also a sanctioned government website. However, what might slightly decrease the validity of the source is that there is no single author cited in the source.

part of a wider drive to maintain western control. It is proven that many western states not only sell arms to these groups, but also provide 'non-lethal assistance' such as body armour, military vehicles, training and logistical support. (Milne, 2016)[10] For what reason does the U.S for doing this? First reports of such action occurred in their intervention of the Soviet invasion of Afghanistan in the 1970's. They trained, armed and radicalized local militias in the hope they would fight against the Soviets. This plan worked; however, problems occurred afterwards due to the spread of these fundamentalist Islamic extremist ideals.

A further source which supports (Milne, 2016) and arguably most atrocious cause of human rights violations in recent history is an article published GlobalResearch.ca. The article states, "Islamic State (ISIS) is made-in-the-USA, an instrument of terror designed to divide and conquer the oil-rich Middle East and to counter Iran's growing influence in the region." (Chengu, 2016)[11i] The article then talks about the Soviet backed nationalist in Afghanistan, which I mentioned beforehand. The article then state "The director if the NSA in the states that in 1978-79 the US tried to pass laws against terrorism, but couldn't as in every version the US would be in violation of its own law!" (Chengu, 2016) The article then gives the numerous examples of this intervention with Islamic extremist groups, such as during the 1970's the CIA used the Muslim Brotherhood in Egypt as a barrier, both to hinder Soviet expansion and prevent the spread of Marxist ideology among the Arab masses.

The two aforementioned sources agree, in that American meddling in international politics has caused a situation, which threatens international security. ISIS and other affiliated groups such as Al-Qaeda, who have since committed numerous terrorist attacks, and have tried to create an Islamic state, which has resulted in them violating the human rights of international citizens to do so. This strongly suggests that America is the biggest threat to international security.

---

[10] A left-wing author, who is a political aide in the Labour party and so will want to portray the right-wing government's actions in the worst possible light, wrote this source, meaning that the source is subject to political bias, as the author has his own political agenda. This results in the reliability of the source being drawn into question.

[11] This source may be unreliable as no credentials of the author are given. Although a search of his name reveals he is of African origin and has graduated from Harvard. He is also a speaker and political activist, so his articles may have some elements of political bias in them, meaning the source may be somewhat unreliable. However, he used credible sources to construct this article, meaning the source will certain have elements of reliability.

Conclusion

Combining all the information that I have collected, I can confidently conclude that America is the biggest threat to international security.

Despite the North Korean governments' use of forced labour and public executions, that enforce harsh restrictions on freedom of information and movement, which are fundamental human rights, such cases do not threaten international security, as these are committed within the DPRK, and not on international citizens, such as the Americans do at Guantanamo bay. Despite some distasteful history under the old regimes, such as selling SCUD missiles to Yemen in 19994 (editors M. , 2017), in relation to my dissertation, these crimes were not committed in the current climate, further adding evidence that North Korea is not the biggest threat to international security currently. In reality, North Korea's military capacity has been vastly over-exaggerated, to try to turn people in western countries against communism and totalitarian dictatorships. The reality is that due to North Korea's limited export capacity and its protection from foreign investment inhibits its economic capacity, meaning that it does not have enough money to pump into its military and sustain its governance, such as the Americans do internationally, to be considered the biggest threat to international security.

Furthermore, the threat from ISIS is not particularly dangerous to international security. This is because despite their aims being to expand in Europe (Adam Witnall, 2015) their rule is little than a disorganised acts of terror and a tribal caliphate attempting to create a state. For this reason, ISIS cannot be considered a threat to world security, as they do not have any form of sustainable economic capacity or governance– as there is no formal form of taxation, no factories, and no export capacity- and so soon will eventually fail as a pseudo-state.

For these reasons, I believe that international security has not been under as much threat as it is today since the cold war due to the USA. The U.N has its security council, which is in charge of determining when and where a UN Peacekeeping operation could be deployed. The only problem is, as I have demonstrated thought out this essay; the U.S dominates the U.N by providing the majority of its funding for several dozen international programs as well as providing the largest proportion of soilders. Therefore, this makes the U.N unlikely to challenge America on various issues, which could be argued to be a threat to international security. Furthermore, the U.S also regularly ignores the U.N in various issues such as the violation of human rights in Guantanamo bay, as shown by Amnesty international is 2016/2017 report on the states: "the UN human rights committee said that the US was obliged to investigate accusations into torture, and it had not taken place." (International, 2017). This clearly shows that America is untrustworthy, does not answer to the U.N and so is easily be the biggest threat to international security.

Furthermore, the estimated number of U.S military bases around the world is 800 (Vine, 2017). For what reason the U.S need so many military bases across the world, in so many countries? In many of the countries, the U.S has its bases in; it has never been at war with, for example Portugal.

It is for the aforementioned reasons that it is clear that America is the biggest threat to international security.

Bibliography

Adam Witnall, D. R. (2015). Isis, a year of the caliphate: What is it that so called 'Islamic state' wants? *Independent.*

Chengu, G. (2016, May 23). *America created the Al-Qaeda and the ISIS Terror group.* Retrieved from Global Research: https://www.globalresearch.ca/america-created-al-qaeda-and-the-isis-terror-group/5402881

cited, N. (2009, 27 April). *U.S. nuclear weapon policy.* Retrieved from CFR: http://www.cfr.org/report/us-nuclear-weapons-policy

cited, N. (2018, February 2). *North Korea.* Retrieved from Human rights watch: https://www.hrw.org/asia/north-korea

Danny Romero, A. W. (2017). Isis, a year of the caliphate: What is it that the so-called 'Islamic State' really wants? *Independent.*

Dearden, L. (2017). *North Korea 'a bigger threat to world peace' than crisis in Syria, British voters say.* Independent.

editors, M. (2017, 10 12). *North Korean and UK relations.* Retrieved from Wikipedia: www.wikipedia.org

editors, M. (2017, 10 10). *Noth Korea and United states relations.* Retrieved from Wikipedia: www.wikipedia.org

Evans, J. D. (2017, September 25). *ISIS reveal 6 reasons why they despise Westerners.* Retrieved from Mirror: http://www.mirror.co.uk/news/world-news/why-isis-hate-you-reasons-8533563

Hammer, J. (2017, February 19). *Which country is the greatest threat to world peace?* Retrieved 10 14, 2017, from Brilliant maps: brilliantmaps.com/threat-to-peace/

International, A. (2017, 09 19). *The United States of America 2016/2017.* Retrieved from Amnesty international: : www.amnesty.org/en/countries/americas/united-states-of-america/report-united-states-of-america/

Milne, S. (2016, April 16). *Now the truth arises, how the US fuellled the rise of ISIS in Iraq and Syria.* Retrieved from the guardian: http://www.the guradian.com

Oxford Dictionary. (Originally 1884). *Oxford english dictionary.* Oxford: Oxford press.

Vine, D. (2017, 10 20). *Where in the world is the U.S military?* Retrieved from Politico: : www.politico.com/magazine/story/2015/06/us-military-bases-around-the-world-119321

YOUR KNOWLEDGE HAS VALUE

- We will publish your bachelor's and master's thesis, essays and papers

- Your own eBook and book - sold worldwide in all relevant shops

- Earn money with each sale

Upload your text at www.GRIN.com and publish for free